LOOKING AT
COUNTRIES

Looking at
ITALY

Jillian Powell

GARETH**STEVENS**
GS
PUBLISHING

A Member of the WRC Media Family of Companies

Please visit our web site at: www.garethstevens.com
For a free color catalog describing Gareth Stevens Publishing's list
of high-quality books and multimedia programs, call 1-800-542-2595 (USA)
or 1-800-387-3178 (Canada). Gareth Stevens Publishing's fax: (414) 332-3567.

Library of Congress Cataloging-in-Publication Data

Powell, Jillian.
    Looking at Italy / Jillian Powell.
       p. cm. — (Looking at countries)
    Includes index.
    ISBN-13: 978-0-8368-7670-3 (lib. bdg.)
    ISBN-13: 978-0-8368-7677-2 (softcover)
    1. Italy—Juvenile literature. I. Title.
  DG417.P683   2006
  945—dc22   2006034464

This North American edition first published in 2007 by
Gareth Stevens Publishing
A Member of the WRC Media Family of Companies
330 West Olive Street, Suite 100
Milwaukee, Wisconsin 53212 USA

This U.S. edition copyright © 2007 by Gareth Stevens, Inc.
Original edition copyright © 2006 by Franklin Watts.
First published in Great Britain in 2006 by Franklin Watts,
338 Euston Road, London NW1 3BH, United Kingdom.

Series editor: Sarah Peutrill
Art director: Jonathan Hair
Design: Rita Storey
Picture research: Diana Morris

Gareth Stevens editor: Dorothy L. Gibbs
Gareth Stevens art direction: Tammy West
Gareth Stevens graphic designer: Charlie Dahl

Photo credits: (t=top, b=bottom, l=left, r=right, c=center)
Age Fotostock/Superstock: 4, 11, 19, 20, 21b. Gaetano Barone/zefa/Corbis: 15. Paul Carr/Photographers Direct: 12.
Bernd Ducke/Superbild/A1 pix: 25. Adam Eastland/Photographers Direct: 10. Kevin Galvin/European Stock Photo/Photographers Direct: 23.
Dallas and John Heaton/Corbis: 27. Lumenstock/Corbis: 16. Stephanie Maze/Corbis: 22. Alberto Pizzoli/Sygma/Corbis: 26b. Olycom Spa/
Rex Features: 24. Vinnie Streano/Corbis: 14b. Eberhard Streichan/zefa/Corbis:18. Superbild/A1 pix: front cover, 1, 6, 7, 8, 17, 21t, 26c.
Geray Sweeney/Corbis: 14t. Richard Wareham/Alamy: 13. Brenton West/Photographers Direct: 9.

Every effort has been made to trace the copyright holders for the photos used in this book. The publisher apologizes,
in advance, for any unintentional omissions and would be pleased to insert the appropriate acknowledgements in any
subsequent edition of this publication.

Printed in Canada

1 2 3 4 5 6 7 8 9 10 10 09 08 07 06

Contents

Words that appear in the glossary are printed in **boldface** type the first time they occur in the text.

Where is Italy?

Italy is in southern Europe. It is a long country surrounded by five seas. The islands of Sicily, Sardinia, and Capri are also part of Italy.

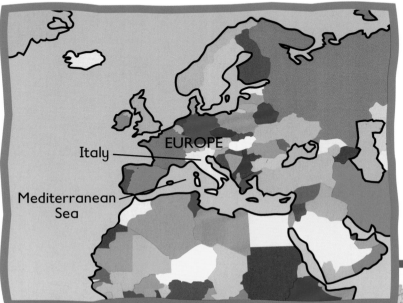

Italy is on a boot-shaped **peninsula** in the **Mediterranean**.

Rome is Italy's capital city. It has many famous buildings, such as the **Colosseum**, from the time of the **Roman Empire**. It also has modern shops and skyscrapers and beautiful parks.

The Spanish steps are one of Rome's famous landmarks.

Did you know?

Italians call Italy *bel paese*, which means "beautiful country."

Northern Italy shares its borders with four other European countries. The high mountains of the Alps are in the northwest, along the borders of France and Switzerland. The Dolomite mountains are in the northeast, along the borders of Switzerland, Austria, and Slovenia.

This map shows all the places that are mentioned in this book.

The Landscape

Italy is famous for its beautiful landscapes and coastlines. The mountains in the north have snow-covered peaks, icy **glaciers**, and **fertile** valleys. Large lakes, such as Lake Como and Lake Garda, can be found in the foothills of the Alps and the Dolomites.

Lake Garda is Italy's largest lake. It is a very popular place for **tourists**.

South of the mountains, Italy has huge areas of flat land and rolling hills. These areas have many rivers and streams so they are good places to grow things. Grapes and olives grow here.

The landscape of Tuscany has many hills.

The landscapes further south, and on the islands of Sardinia and Sicily, are rough and mountainous. Southern Italy has three **volcanoes**: Mount Vesuvius, near the city of Naples; Mount Etna on the island of Sicily; and the island volcano of Stromboli.

Did you know?

Mount Etna is the largest volcano in Europe.

Weather and Seasons

The weather in northern Italy is cooler and wetter than in southern Italy. In autumn, heavy rains can cause flooding.

In northern Italy, heavy snowfalls begin as early as October.

In the mountains of northern Italy, summers are short, and winters are very cold, with a lot of heavy snow. The highest mountain peaks are snow-covered all through the year. A strong wind called the Bora blows across northeastern Italy in the winter months.

Did you know?

In Trieste, people put stones on the roofs of their houses to keep the Bora from blowing the roof tiles away.

Southern Italy's warm, sunny weather attracts tourists to beaches such as this one in Positano.

Most of southern Italy has Mediterranean weather, with hot, dry summers, mild winters, and some rain in spring and autumn. In the far south, and on the islands of Sicily and Sardinia, the weather is almost always hot and dry. In summer, these areas sometimes have **droughts**.

Italian People

Italy has twenty different regions, and each region has its own traditional foods, **folk costumes**, festivals, and **dialects**. Besides speaking Italian dialects, some Italians living in border regions also speak other languages, such as French, German, or Greek.

These Italian women are wearing folk costumes for a festival in Rome.

Thousands of people gather on Sundays in St. Peter's Square, in **Vatican City**, for the Pope's Catholic church services.

The religion of most Italians is Roman Catholic, but Italy also has people who belong to the Protestant, Jewish, or Muslim religions. About one-third of Italy's Catholics go to church regularly, and most celebrate important family and religious events by going to church.

Did you know?

Vatican City is the world's smallest independent, or self-ruling, state.

School and Family

Most children in Italy go to school between the ages of six and fifteen. Some children are in school six days a week, from Monday through Saturday. Their classes start at 8:30 a.m. and end at 1:00 p.m. For other children, school days are Monday through Friday, from 8:30 a.m. to 4:30 p.m., with a lunch break.

At some Italian schools, students wear uniforms, or special clothing that helps people know which school they are from.

These families in Venice are enjoying some time together outdoors on a sunny evening.

Families and home life are important to Italians. Relatives often share in the care of the children and enjoy celebrating family events together. When Italian families eat out, the whole family, including the young children, goes along — even when it is late in the evening.

Country Life

The Italian countryside has many old villages and hill towns that have changed very little over hundreds of years. Most Italians in countryside areas still live in old-fashioned ways. Some work as farmers. Others just keep a few pigs and chickens to have meat and eggs.

Italian farmers grow grapes, grains, potatoes, sugar beets, and olives. They also raise cows and other farm animals.

This man is harvesting olives in Tuscany.

Grapes have been grown in Italy since Roman times.

Baskets, woven bags, and pottery are some of the crafts for sale on the street in this Apulia village. Apulia is the region that forms Italy's "heel."

As more and more tourists visit Italy's historic country towns and villages, fewer people living in these places work as farmers. Many people now have jobs in hotels and cafes. Others make crafts, which they sell from their homes or at local markets. Some of the houses in country villages are now vacation homes for Italians or tourists.

Did you know?

Bears and wolves live wild in the hills of Calabria. This region forms the "toe" of Italy.

City Life

Most Italians live in cities or towns near cities. Many live in the **suburbs** and travel each day to city centers to work. Except for Naples, the main industrial cities are in central and northern Italy. Busy cities such as Rome, Milan, Turin, and Genoa have factories, banks, offices, and shops. Milan is known worldwide for its designer fashion shops.

Motorbikes and electric trolleys, or streetcars, are common sights on many of Italy's busy city streets.

The city of Venice is built on islands in a **lagoon** so most city steets are **canals** instead of roads.

Millions of tourists from all over the world visit Italy's cities. The capital city of Rome has many famous buildings and landmarks, including St. Peter's **Basilica** and the Colosseum. Venice and Florence are also popular cities with beautiful buildings, churches, art galleries, and museums.

Did you know?

Italy has more than three thousand museums.

Italian Houses

In cities, towns, and suburbs, most Italians live in apartment buildings. Some of the older apartment buildings are only a few stories high. Other apartment buildings are newly built towers.

Many Italian apartments have overhanging porches, or balconies. The balconies are nice for sitting out in the fresh air, but some Italians also find them useful for hanging laundry out to dry.

These old stone houses are in the hill town of San Gimignano, in Tuscany.

In the countryside, more people live in houses than in apartment buildings. The older country houses are usually built of stone and have clay-tiled roofs.

In the Apulia region, the houses in some villages have a special design. They are round, white buildings with rounded, or dome-shaped, stone roofs.

Italian Food

Italy is known all over the world for its food and cooking. Each region is proud of its own special foods and dishes, such as salami from Bologna and cannoli from Sicily.

Pizza and pasta are popular Italian foods. There are hundreds of kinds of pasta, and each region has its own pasta dishes and sauces.

This man in Tuscany is making fresh pasta.

In Bologna, the fresh fish market is a popular place.

Most Italians shop for food at supermarkets, but they also buy fresh foods from street markets and small stores such as butcher shops and bakeries. Italians often use fresh local foods, including olive oil, tomatoes, vegetables, and seasonings, to cook their regional dishes.

Espresso is a popular drink in Italy. It is very strong coffee served in a small cup.

At Work

In Italian cities and towns, people work in offices, banks, shops, and factories. Italy has many different industries, especially in the northern regions. Italian factories make foods, machinery, iron and steel, cars, and clothes.

These women are making leather shoes in a factory near Milan.

Italy has a busy tourist industry. Nearly forty million tourists visit Italy each year to enjoy the food and to see the beautiful countryside and lakes, as well as the historic cities. Tourism provides many jobs for Italians in restaurants and hotels and at all the country's visitor attractions.

This man works as a waiter at an ice cream cafe in Rome. Italy's ice cream, or gelato, is world famous.

Did you know?

Italy is the fourth most visited country in the world.

Having Fun

Most Italians enjoy sports. Soccer, cycling, auto racing, basketball, and skiing are all popular sports in Italy.

Italians also enjoy the arts, including art shows, theater, movies, and **operas**. La Scala, in Milan, is the most famous opera house in the world.

The Grand Prix is a world-famous auto race held every year near Milan.

People dress up in costumes and wear masks for Carnival. This festival is held every year, in February.

There are colorful festivals in all parts of Italy at all times of the year. Some of these festivals celebrate Christian holidays or saints' days. Others celebrate the harvests of foods such as wheat and wild mushrooms. Italians dress up for many of the festivals and often have street parades or races. In summer, there is a famous horse race, called the Palio, through the streets of Siena.

Italy: The Facts

- Italy is a **republic**. The president is the **head of state**, and the prime minister leads the government.

- Italy is divided into twenty different regions. Five of the regions, including Sardinia and Sicily, have their own governments.

- Italy is a member of the European Union.

The Italian flag has bands of green, white, and red.

Italian currency is the euro. It is the same currency used by many other countries in the European Union.

This huge cathedral is in Milan, Italy's second largest city.

- More than fifty-eight million people live in Italy.

- Italy's largest cities are Rome, Milan, Naples, and Turin.

- More than three million people live in Rome.

Glossary

basilica – a very large Christian church

canals – narrow waterways

Carnival – a colorful celebration held right before the start of Lent, which is a Christian time of sorrow before Easter

Colosseum – a large, open-air stadium, now in ruins, that was built in ancient Rome and was used for fights and contests

dialects – local ways of speaking languages

droughts – long periods of time without rain that are harmful to plants and animals in the area

fertile – having rich soil that is good for growing crops

folk costumes – special kinds of clothing that are passed down through generations in a particular country

glaciers – large masses of ice that can cover wide areas

head of state – the main representative of a country

lagoon – a small, shallow body of water that is near or connected to a large, deep body of water

Mediterranean – the name used to describe all the lands and waters that border the Mediterranean Sea

operas – musical plays in which all words are sung, not spoken

peninsula – a strip of land that sticks out into a body of water and is surrounded by water on three sides

republic – a kind of government in which decisions are made by the people of the country and their representatives

Roman Empire – the lands ruled by the ancient city of Rome from 31 B.C. until the fifth century A.D.

suburbs – areas outside of large cities, made up mostly of homes where people live, instead of places where people work

tourists – people who visit a place mainly to see its sights and to enjoy all the special things the place has to offer

Vatican City – a separate state within Rome, where the Pope, who is the leader of the Roman Catholic church, lives and carries out church business

volcanoes – mountains formed by the dust, ashes, and melted rock that hot gases deep underground have caused to explode through Earth's crust

Find Out More

Enchanted Learning: Italy
www.enchantedlearning.com/europe/italy/

Italy (Italia) for Kids
www2.lhric.org/pocantico/italy/italy.htm

A Kid's Life in Italy
library.thinkquest.org/CR0212302/italy.html

Publisher's note to educators and parents: Our editors have carefully reviewed these Web sites to ensure that they are suitable for children. Many Web sites change frequently, however, and we cannot guarantee that a site's future contents will continue to meet our high standards of quality and educational value. Be advised that children should be closely supervised whenever they access the Internet.

My Map of Italy

Photocopy or trace the map on page 31. Then write in the names of the regions, cities, mountains, islands, and bodies of water listed below. (Look at the map on page 5 if you need help.)

After you have written in the names of all the places, find some crayons and color the map!

Regions
Apulia
Basilicata
Calabria
Tuscany

Cities
Bologna
Florence
Genoa
Milan
Naples
Positano
Rome
San Gimignano
Siena
Trieste
Turin
Vatican City
Venice

Mountains
Alps
Dolomites
Mount Etna
Mount Vesuvius

Islands
Capri
Sardinia
Sicily
Stromboli

Bodies of Water
Adriatic Sea
Ionian Sea
Ligurian Sea
Mediterranean Sea
Tyrrhenian Sea
Lake Como
Lake Garda

Index